Eskdale Way

An 82 mile circular walk in the North York Moors National Park

by

Louis S. Dale

Dalesman Books
1983

The Dalesman Publishing Company Ltd.,
Clapham, via Lancaster, LA2 8EB

First published 1983
© Louis S. Dale 1983

ISBN: 0 85206 744 5

DEDICATED TO CATHLEEN

Printed by Alf Smith & Co., Bradford

Contents

Cover photograph of Beckhole by Jack Wetherby.

Line drawings in the text by E. Gower, Elizabeth Gray, Albert Walker and Alec E. F. Wright.

Maps by E. Gower.

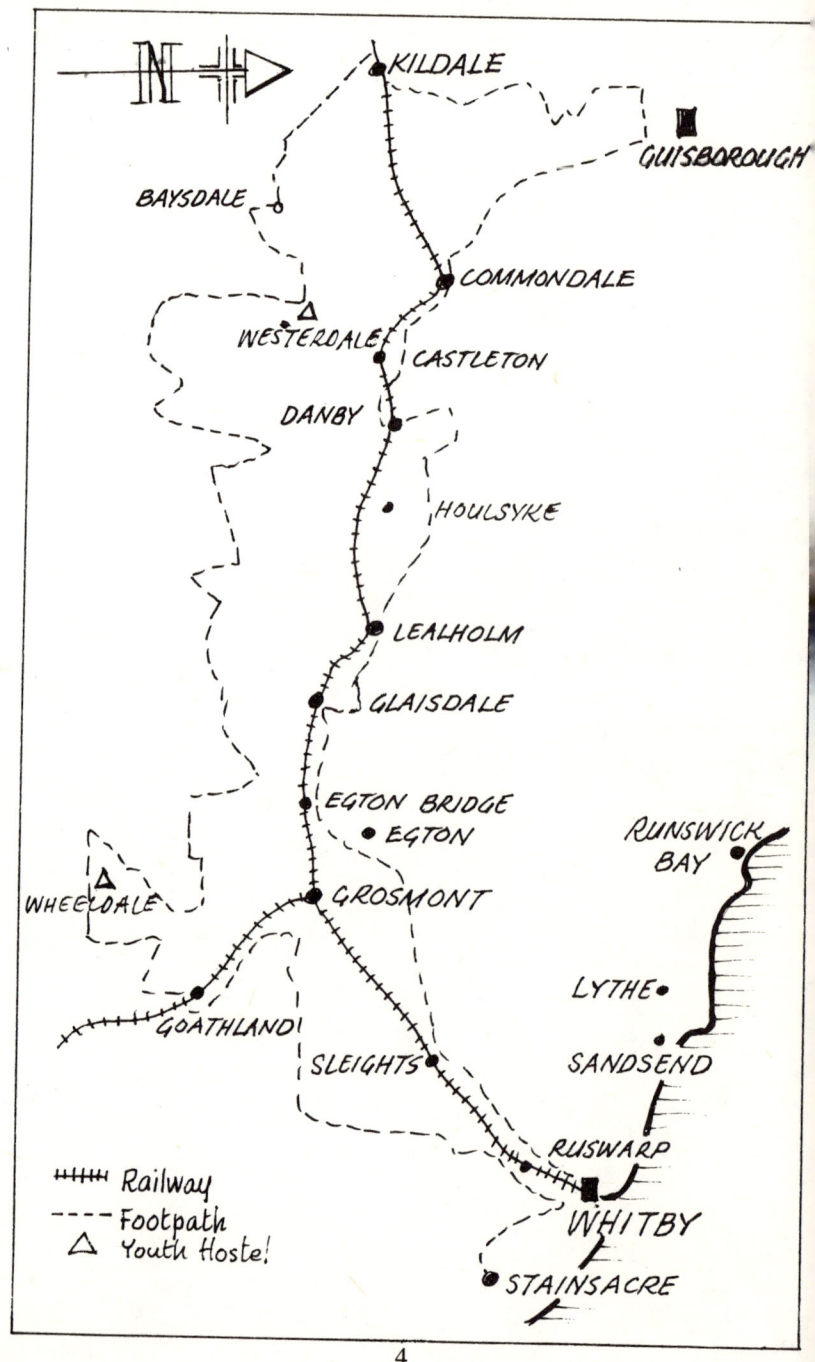

Introduction

FOR some time now I have been pondering as to whether to put pen to paper and write a detailed route of a long distance walk round Eskdale. I have now made up my mind, so here goes. The moors, fields, woodland and the country lanes of the valley of the Esk have been my pleasure for quite a number of years and I would claim to know them reasonably well. Others in the past have written of the splendours of this area and have described routes for its walks, but I feel that an area of such unique beauty, though comparatively small, deserves to have its own named way. In distance it is of no great length, 82 miles in all. If I had made deeper incursions into the moors it would have ceased to have been known as the Eskdale Way.

In my approach I have tried to incorporate all that is best in this area and have therefore made some loop diversions off the main valley. The farthest distance that I have erred from the River Esk is to Highcliff Nab, as the crow flies just under 5½ miles. I felt that the Guisborough and Commondale Moors could just not be left out.

In planning the route I have experienced difficulties in making it tie in so that the distance between the route and accommodation was not too great. Where there has been a tussle between accommodation and the moors, I am afraid that the moors have won. There is also a definite shortage of accommodation in some areas, notably Westerdale, Baysdale and Danby. Strong walkers will not find too much difficulty, they will just push on if needs be. I have tried to think of others, the older walker and those with young families, I would like them to enjoy the walk too. For those who intend to camp overnight I have very little to offer in the way of camping sites. I presume that some farmers will oblige if they are approached politely.

I have based a chapter on a day's walking, that is my day's walking and not necessarily yours. Bear in mind when planning your walk, the distance involved in going off the route for accommodation and the return journey to get back on to the route the following morning. If you take as an example that you are in the head of Fryup Dale, 3 to 3½ miles of walking will be required to get to Ainthorpe or Danby. Or, if you are in the region of Ralphs Cross, 4½ miles has to be added to the day's walking to get to Castleton. I would not hesitate to add that this road walking for accommodation is in excellent country and can be enjoyed to the full. In some instances you do not have to stick to the roads; good paths can be found on the Ordnance Survey maps and these can be tried as an alternative. There is the possibility of arranging with a taxi service, but this will add to your expenses.

I may have gone into quite a deal of detail in describing my route, but personally I find it quite disconcerting when following a routed walk and the details are sketchy. You can spend too much of your time concentrating on which way you are intended to go and then sorting yourself out if you have come to the wrong decision. It takes away a lot of the pleasure. In order to break up the tedium of reading a never-ending continuous route, I have incorporated odd anecdotes, history, whether it be fact or fiction, which may help to make the story more interesting.

As regards the footpaths I have only taken those that are shown on the Ordnance Survey maps, Whitby, Sheet 94, 1:50,000 second series, and the Danby and Eskdale, Sheet NZ 60/70, as rights-of-way; or where there is no right-of-way, the owners allow passage as a concession.

An accommodation list is available from the author providing an addressed and stamped envelope is forwarded. It would be wise to write or telephone before embarking on the walk, especially as to whether an evening meal is available. I also include a little information on bus and train services which could be of help for those without their own transport. More detailed information can be obtained from the offices of the respective transport companies concerned.

I am not making reference as to what to wear as regards clothing or footwear; sufficient has been said of that subject in other books, periodicals and leaflets. I would emphasize, however, that unless you are camping, if your rucksack weighs over 30 lbs., you are carrying too much.

Make preparation before hand. If you cannot get out distance walking regularly, have a few training trips prior to commencing the walk. If you happen to have new boots, do break them in before hand. If you are properly prepared I see no reason why you should not obtain as much pleasure and enjoyment as I do.

— **Louis S. Dale,**
10 Mulgrave View,
Stainsacre, Whitby,
North Yorkshire YO22 4NX.

1. Whitby to Darnholm

IF you are going to walk the valley of the Esk what finer way of doing it than making the walk circuitous. This prompts the question as to where to start from. To me the answer is simple, what could be more suitable than Whitby itself? Positioned right at the very mouth of the river, a good place to start and finish with every amenity available with transport facilities, shops, accommodation and to suit all pockets.

The ideal place to start the walk is Station Square, where bus and train rendezvous. When you are satisfied that you have all that you require in the way of shopping (shops are few once you have left Whitby), turn along New Quay Road. Cross the swing bridge, then turn left down Church Street. As you walk along there is plenty to catch the eye in the form of river activity. Fishermen work at their nets on the quay side or in their cobles. Ships from foreign ports may be seen unloading their merchandise, or slowly turning on their axis as they prepare to dock. As you cross the swing bridge and look down towards the piers a mass of masts will be seen where the keel boats are tied up. Pleasure craft ply up and down as Whitby now has a marina which is fast growing in popularity. If it is at the weekend when you begin your walk you will most likely see long shallow racing boats; their crew of four with oars and a cox bend their backs in training effort. Whitby has two rowing clubs which have a great but friendly rivalry with each other.

Turning down Church Street the small shops will capture your gaze as they ply their many and varied products. The old town is interesting and will captivate your imagination as you walk down its narrow streets. Many things are to be seen like Chomley's old town hall, the market place alongside; but the market has not always been sited there. At the end of Church Street you have the choice of climbing the 199 steps or walking up the steeply cobbled Donkey Road, passing at the top the memorial to Caedmon, England's first known poet, immediately followed by St. Mary's Church. This church must be the most unusual and at the same time the most interesting parish church in the whole of England. The remains of Aldwin's magnificent abbey church which stands on the site of the older abbey of St. Hilda is over on your right.

On coming out on to the Abbey Plain, make your way diagonally to the cliff top near the Coast Guard station. Before stepping out along the cliff top footpath, stop and look back at the fine view of the town laid out before you — the West Cliff with its fine clean beach sweeping away towards Sandsend which can just be seen in the distance, the mass of Sandsend Ness jutting out into the sea, the top of the steeple of St. Oswald's Church at Lythe, just protruding above the woods of Mulgrave. Let your gaze wander inland and you will see the great expanse of moors folding away into the distance. You will see more of these fine moors as you continue your walk and will come to a more intimate understanding with them.

Let us proceed just for a couple of miles along this fine cliff top path, a small section of the designated Heritage Coast. It would be a pity not to enjoy just a little of this fine cliff top walk and we are only going to wander a short distance from our main objective — the valley of the Esk. The sea catches your eye irrespective of its mood, it draws you like a magnet. Plenty of sea birds are to be seen on the rocks below and on the cliff ledges. Herring gulls and black headed gulls are the most numerous, but other varieties can be seen — great blacked backed gulls, cormorants, shags, common gulls and fulmars. If the tide be out, quite a variety of waders can be seen, such as dunlin, redshanks, oyster catchers, sandpipers and others. Another breed of bird not normally associated with the sea shore is here in quite large numbers, jackdaws. These birds like a cliff habitat whether it be inland or on the coast. If you look carefully during the summer you will see holes in the boulder clay at the top of the cliffs; these are where the sand martins make their nests. Other birds seen on the cliff top are wheatears, a bird of the moors; they love to play leap frog along the tops of stone walls. Kestrels can be seen hovering as they hunt for a meal

A good job of work has been carried out along this coastal path in that lengths of duck boards, steps and bridges have been erected in the muddiest places. It is certainly a boon to walkers. After walking about a mile you come to the Saltwick Bay holiday village, your path passing right through the centre. If already you feel like taking refreshment, the village walk-round store will cater for you. As you pass out of the holiday village a good stretch of sand can be seen below in the small bay between Saltwick Nab and Black Nab.

Saltwick Bay has obviously obtained its name from the mining of salt — the crystalline alum salt which has been mined and quarried along this coast from about the end of the 16th century. The first mine to open was actually a few miles inland at Belman Bank near Guisborough. Other mines quickly followed along the coast, at Loftus, Boulby, Kettleness, Sandsend and Saltwick. Other mines opened inland in other parts of the northern end of the moors. An alum shale heap is to be seen in the woods between Littlebeck and Falling Foss. Mining of alum shale started at Saltwick in 1649 and carried on through the years with varying measures of prosperity, finally closing in the year 1791. During this period of time, the mining, processing and distribution of alum employed quite a few hundred people in Whitby and its surrounding area. Shortly after the

The roofs of Whitby.

mine was opened a harbour was constructed to take small boats which transported the alum by sea, mainly to London, although some was exported overseas to Europe. If the tide is out, a small number of squared stones neatly placed can be seen below. I do not know, but have wondered if these are the remains of a small section of the old harbour. During this period of quarrying and mining the coast line has been altered considerably. I understand that originally there was little or nothing which you could say represented a bay.

Another point of interest while you are in this area is the wreck of the *Admiral Von Tromp,* a Scarborough keel boat which went aground one night on the nab. Two men lost their lives and two were saved by the superb efforts of the inshore lifeboat, police and coastguard service. It may be of interest that the name of the boat is in remembrance of the famous Dutch Admiral of that name. The boat went aground on rocks at the rear of Black Nab in September 1976, but in the storm which ravaged the north-east coast on the night of February 1st, 1983, it was wrested from the rocks and washed an estimated distance of 50 yards to the foot of the cliffs.

We must press on for a further mile of pleasant walking to the fog warning station and the lighthouse. If you are unfortunate enough to be walking when there is a sea fret and the fog horn is sounding, be careful that you gauge the passing below the fog horn between signals, otherwise you may find it quite distressing.

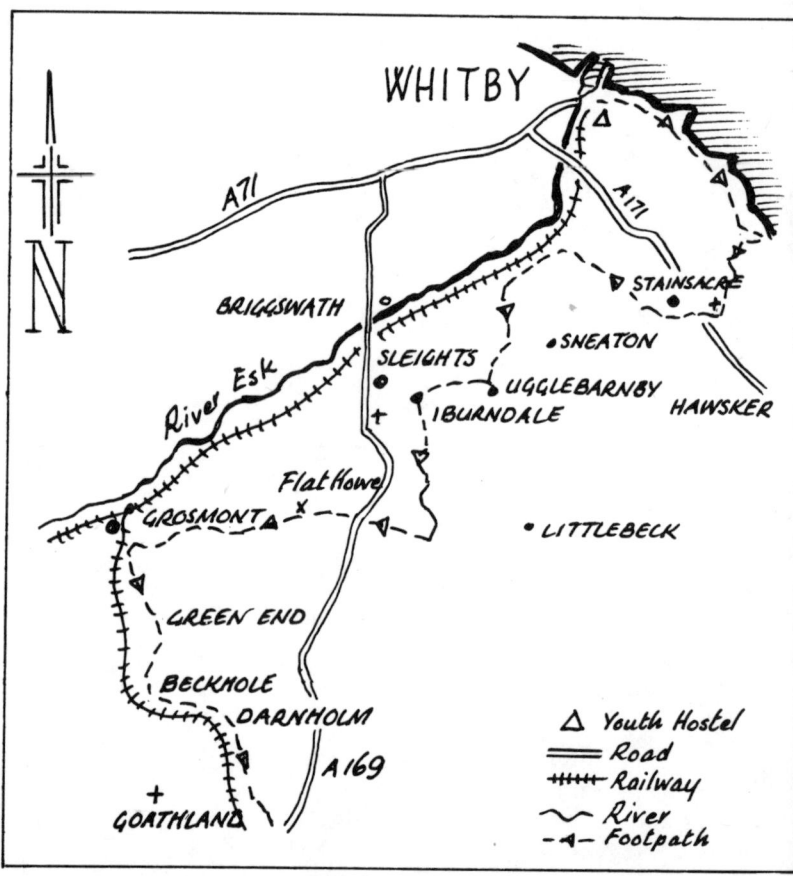

Having passed in front of the fog horn station, climb the stile and cross over the pasture diagonally to the far corner. Negotiate another stile on to the metalled road in front of the main gate of the lighthouse. Turn right up this road and on reaching the first cottage on a bend, go through a field gate on your left and cross the small paddock to another gate. Pass through and follow the fence up the right-hand side. This field narrows at the top and a further gate takes you out on to a farm track. Very shortly you pass the farm house, Beacon Hill, closely followed by the farm, Whitby Laithes. Just past the latter farm you come to a T junction with another farm track. Turn right and within 30 yards you will come to a field gate on your left. Pass through and follow track to the end of the field. Here you turn right and follow the hedge down till you come to the road, known as Hawsker Lane. Turn left and proceed towards the church which can be seen ahead.

Just past the church a road turns off to the right; follow this road for a quarter of a mile until you meet the main road, the A171. Cross this road and carry on into Stainsacre village. On reaching the sharp right hand turn in the village, cross over the road and go straight ahead as if to go to Stainsacre Hall. On the driveway coming out into a field, cross the field diagonally to the far corner where a stepping stile will take you over a wall into a second field. Go straight ahead aiming for the trees in the dip at the far end. A stile takes you into Scraper Lane. Turn left, you will find it rough, stony and in the main wet. Shortly this lane will bring you down to Stainsacre Beck. Cross the footbridge and climb upwards; any of the paths will bring you out of the woods on to the broad lane which runs along the ridge of Long Rigg. Turn right and follow this lane.

Shortly the track becomes metalled; you pass first a bungalow and then Golden Rigg Farm. The track now begins to drop and after passing what used to be the *Golden Grove Hotel* the road turns to the left, a bridge taking it over Cock Mill Beck. Do not follow the road, keep straight on past some stables and at the end the path narrows and drops steeply down through the trees by Waterfall Cottage. It has been quite pleasant walking along here and it is worth stopping and taking a few moments' rest to observe this quite idyllic setting. The cottage, garden and the waterfall should be an artist's or photographer's delight. The waterfall looks good, or at least I think so; it can roar when the beck is in full spate.

It is now very pleasant walking as we pass through these woods with the beck tumbling along by your side. The trees are many and varied: sycamore, beech, oak, maple, snowberry, elder, holly and occasional silver birch. Rhododendrons are to be seen scattered among these trees, a picture in the month of June. At the point where Stainsacre Beck joins Cock Mill Beck a footbridge crosses the beck on your left. This path climbs up and twists through the trees, passing through sylvan glades before coming to high hedges which take it to the village of Sneaton. Much of this path is made up of paved stones and is generally referred to as the monks' trod. However, this is not our path for today, but it is well worth remembering for another time.

We keep straight on and as we begin to climb we now have another of these paved trods. The whole of this northern end of the North York Moors is well covered with these paved causeways and you will keep coming across them in the side roads, lanes, woods and across fields. Prior to the middle of the eighteenth century all roads leading into Whitby were very rough tracks over the moors. They were difficult to traverse at times in summer and nigh impossible in winter. Obviously the monks would have a need for paths and tracks to facilitate travel but it is generally accepted that these paved causeways were of a later period of time. In general the causeway was to help the man's progress over rough terrain and his pack horse had

11

to make the best of what there was in the form of a track alongside.

It is also of interest while on the walk in this Golden Grove area to mention about Captain Scoresby senior's pet polar bear. Captain Scoresbys, both father and son, were famous whaling sea captains of the late 18th and early 19th centuries. In this time they sailed out of Whitby for the Arctic seas to catch whales, seals and other Arctic life which was of beneficial use. On one occasion he brought back a young polar bear which he apparently tamed. He normally kept it chained up near a corner of Spital Bridge in Whitby. On this occasion it was found wandering loose in Cock Mill Woods much to the consternation of the local inhabitants. Captain Scoresby was contacted and taking a noosed rope went to collect the bear. Placing the noose over its head he led it away as anyone else would lead a dog.

This path eventually comes out on to a metalled road. You join it near the top of Danger Bank, turning left and walking down towards Glen Esk and the caravan site of the same name. You now have the company of the River Esk until you join the main road, B1416, at Ruswarp.

On joining this road turn left and continue along by the Ruswarp auction mart. Just past the mart you begin to climb steeply up Oakley Bank, but only for about 60 yards. Here you turn right down a lane which has a miscellany of habitations. Shortly you come to a crossing over the Middlesbrough/Whitby railway line. Cross here, but beware of trains, they are still running on this line. On crossing you bear to the left. You now have the railway on your left and the Esk on your right just a small field away. On passing through a field gate keep straight on until you come opposite Brickyard House near the end of the field. Here you re-cross the railway; don't forget to look for trains. Having crossed safely bear right and climb up the steepish slope. At the top stop for a rest and look back to take in the view. It is a fine view with the old Whitby Abbey as a centre piece.

When rested follow the bend round to the left and you will shortly come to Hagg House. The farm buildings are still in use, although the old farm house has been pulled down in recent years; a new house is in the process of being built. You are now faced with three field gates, the one on your left is a little way over and is ignored. Take the centre gate and go straight ahead keeping the hedge on your left. Since leaving the B1416 there are no signposts or way markers but you should not have had much difficulty. At the top of this field pass through an opening into the next one and bear to the right for a few yards then keep the hedge on your right; a stile is crossed into the following field.

You have been steadily climbing all this time and if you stop and turn you will see that your distant view has widened out bringing Briggswath into view on your left. On coming to the top of this field you come to a metalled road; cross over where the footpath sign is

12

positioned. Now on the road turn right and walk downhill towards Ugglebarnby. Fine extensive views are to be seen as you travel downhill all the way to Iburndale. You will shortly pass Tinkler Hall on your right –– an unusual name and quite old according to the date stone. On coming to the lower end of Ugglebarnby you come to a T-junction; turn right here and it drops you directly down to the hamlet of Iburndale.

A short distance down the hill you come to a bench seat; this makes a good stopping place for a rest and to take in the view. Looking over, you can see the road ascending Blue Bank and out beyond over the moor. On the roads we have travelled so far, traffic in general has been quite light, except for the ¼ mile on the B1416. In the whole of this walk I have tried to keep road walking to a minimum, but in nearly all cases it is pleasant walking in fine country.

Rested, we set off once more dropping down into Iburndale, a most picturesque hamlet with its mixture of old and new cottages and houses. On coming to Mill Lane which is on your left, turn down here, it is signposted as a footpath. Keep straight on to Zetland House, pass through the wicket gate and follow the path down the side of the house. Next cross a stile into a small pasture, into a second pasture this bringing you alongside Little Beck. This is a lovely walk through fields of grazing cattle with the Little Beck singing to you as it travels along. A third field is crossed, still keep the beck on your right. On coming to where the beck swings to the left and enters a small plantation, cross the stile and bear left with the beck. In a few yards you will come to a signpost, turn right and cross the beck by a metal footbridge. Follow the path to the left through the trees and within 120 yards you will come to a field gate. Turn right passing through the gate, a second gate being passed through just prior to coming to the cottage named 'Throstle's Nest'. On reaching the signpost, bear to the left round the cottage, a further 100 yards will bring you to a stile on your right which takes you into a small paddock. Cross the

paddock, then the footbridge over the beck turning right on the narrow metalled road.

You next cross the water splash keeping straight on along the road and shortly passing 'Alum House'. No doubt this house has had connections with the alum industry of years gone by. On reaching the T-junction, turn left along the Littlebeck road. After passing Spring Farm on your right the road takes a sharp turn to the left. At this point a track which is signposted turns off on your right. Carry on up this track, it is steepish and eventually leads on to the moor. You are now actually walking on part of the Coast to Coast Walk and will remain so until you turn off at Low Fairhead.

Where the main track bears sharply to the left, a greener branch track is seen to turn off to your right. Take this latter track which shortly veers off to the left and up the moor. Eventually this track reaches the A169 Whitby/Pickering road. Cross the road, and in 20 yards distance is a signpost and a track leading over the moor to Flat Howe. The Land Rover track shortly narrows down to a single track but it is quite easy to follow to the Grosmont road.

On reaching the road you have two choices; either keep on the road down to the cattle grid, or take the Coast to Coast route visiting the High and Low Bride Stones. The path from the Low Bride Stones comes out back on to the road shortly before the cattle grid. Continue down the road ignoring the farm road on the left which leads to High Fair Head and take the next farm road to Low Fair Head. You have now walked approximately 11¼ miles and if you are thinking of accommodation for the night ⅓ mile will bring you down into Grosmont.

If you are to continue you will pass the bungalow, Moor End, which is on your left, this being followed by Low Fair Head on your right. Keep straight on past this farm crossing over a stile; you now bear half right, this leading to a solitary gate stoup on the other side of the field. Pass the gate stoup and turn down a wide track leading into another pasture. Looking to your right and straight down the grassy slope a stile will be seen giving entry to Lyth Beck Plantation. Cross the stile, the path goes down steeply but you are assisted by some stone steps. Cross the footbridge at the bottom; the beck is quite attractive as it tumbles on its way through the wood. Your climb up the other side is again assisted by stone steps and you come out of the plantation over a stile into a pasture.

Cross this pasture diagonally to your right aiming for the end of the plantation. As you cross so the path will be picked up once more. Just past the end of the plantation the path steepens and you shortly come out on to a metalled road, passing between some timber fencing which incorporates a concrete drinking trough. Turn right down this road and travelling downhill you will shortly come to a footpath sign on your left. A paved trod leads the way to a stile and a gate which gives entrance to Crag Cliff Wood. The track is now quite broad and easy to follow. Watch out for a branch track on your right but ignore it and keep straight on. This is lovely woodland walking and if you happen to be passing this way in the month of June, you will find the bluebells quite entrancing.

You emerge from this wood by a footbridge and a double stile into a field. Keep straight on with the wood still on your right-hand side. Cross two more fields and then enter the wood by a stile. The path curves very sharply to the left and in only a few yards another stile takes you into another field. You now have Spring Wood on your left. As you walk through these woods and fields you will find exceptionally fine views between the breaks in the trees, looking over to Lease Rigg and Esk Valley below.

On crossing this field you will find yourself once more among the trees. The track is now quite broad, but most of the year it is exceptionally muddy. Just prior to coming out of this wood the way bears to the right and over a bridge. Rising sharply you come out at a T-junction, a field gate on your left leads into an enclosed lane. Turn down this lane, which can be quite muddy but incorporates a paved trod. This lane leads to Green End. On reaching the farm bear to the left of it; on passing through two gates you come out on to the road in Green End. You have now walked about 12½ miles and may be thinking of somewhere to sleep for the night. A further two miles' walk will bring you out a ¼ mile from Goathland railway station. Or, you can turn off the route at Darnholme.

To continue the walk follow the short road length from Green End to the T-junction, turning right and walking down towards Beckhole. On coming to the farm track on the left just short of the railway bridge, turn up here for Hill House Farm. If you wish to visit Beck Hole, one of the most attractive hamlets in Britain, it is only a short distance down the 1 in 4 bank. Refreshments can be obtained at the inn.

Passing Hill House Farm on the left, keep to the wall and fence on your right. The path is well defined and brings you to that most delightful place, Darnholm. Drop down the steep slope into the valley below and the stepping stones over the beck. You have now completed 14½ miles.

2. Darnholm to Egton Bridge

AT the bottom of the valley turn to the left passing in front of a fairly large house; the Eller Beck is kept on your right. Go straight ahead climbing the steep path out of the valley. Once at the top keep going straight ahead; the beck and the North Yorkshire Moors railway runs parallel with you in the valley below. On nearing Goathland railway station the path veers away to half left; at this stage you will see the roof tops of some cottages ahead. Shortly your path joins another path of greater width; turn right and follow this path which continues to the road. On coming to the road, turn left and within 100 yards you will see a farm track on your right.

Turn down here and you will eventually cross a cattle grid; still carry on past Partridge Hill Farm. Just below the farm you ford a very shallow beck; pass through the field gate and turn to the right. Keep straight on and after passing the main entrance to Birchwood Farm (note the farm name executed with horse shoes of differing size) the path joins the metalled road. Just prior to meeting the Goathland road you will pass a stone memorial to a local man who passed away some decades ago at this spot.

On reaching the road turn to your right and walk towards Goathland. About half a mile along on your left-hand side, a short distance beyond the farm track to Thornhill, is a public right-of-way over the moor to Simon Howe. It was my intention to take this path, but I found great difficulty in tracing the entry point. The path is undefined most of the way and so there appears to be no alternative, unless you take a compass bearing, but to continue along the road to Goathland.

On reaching the road junction just past Goathland church, turn left and within 200 yards you will see a path on the left which crosses the moor. You will shortly come to a large pond and, as your path approaches, it veers away to the left. This path leads to Two Howes. The path passes below and then away from the second howe and is eventually joined on your left by the path that I had hoped to use from near Thornhill. Turn right and keep straight on up a ridge with a large cairn on the top; this the site of Simon Howe. At this point the route of the Lyke Wake Walk passes in front of you; turn to the right and follow it for about a mile. As you approach Wheeldale Beck the path drops steeply, it is well strewn with rocks and stones. Over on your right is the Wheeldale Youth Hostel, remember this when considering accommodation.

Cross the beck by the stepping stones and then make the steep ascent up to the Roman road. Cross the road and them make your way straight ahead to the stile giving access to the Stape road. Here we take leave of the Lyke Wake Walk, turning right and heading downhill, this bringing you to the popular picnic area in Wheeldale Gill.

Crossing the beck climb up the steep twisting road and just beyond a sharp bend take the path turning off to the right. Shortly your path passes to the left of a hut and joins a track of greater width which leads to a farm gate and a rough pasture. Cross this pasture; the farm Hazel Head can be seen over on your right. Pass through another field gate on to the metalled farm road turning left. After passing Hollin House Farm, you come to a junction with the Goathland/Egton Bridge road opposite the farm known as Julian Park. Turn left and immediately along the edge of the farm buildings will be seen a walled lane. Take this lane which bears to the left on leaving the farm.

The 2½ in. Ordnance Survey maps show a couple of hundred yards to the rear of this farm house as being the site of a castle. According to research into medieval times there never was a castle at Julian Park. Peter de Mauley, the second Baron of Mulgrave, had a hunting lodge at Julian Park during the early 14th century. It is not known how the Park part of the name came about, as Julian Park was not in a park, it was a warren. Parks only came into being by a royal grant. A warren was used for the hunting of small game only. In the year 1294 reference was made to it being named St. Julians. Probably the stones of this old hunting lodge were used to build the present day farm house and outbuildings.

After a few hundred yards the track opens out into a rough pasture. Almost immediately the fence on your left turns at an angle to the left; turn with the fence and follow it to the end of the field. Here there is a sudden steepish drop which brings you to a timber barred entrance leading into Carr Wood.

Cross into the wood and within a hundred yards the path divides. Take the turn to the left, it climbs a little. After a while a further left-hand turn is made. As you turn you can see the fields just beyond the edge of the wood; the gateway is again barred across with timber. Cross the barred gateway, turning right follow the fence and the edge of the wood. You shortly re-enter the wood and then pass through a wicket gate. It is now quite steepish in parts but fortunately it is downhill. It can be quite muddy too due to the passage of horses; it is a designated bridleway. At one stage you have a paved trod which is not too even, many of the paved stones being lopsided and slippy. After a while you come to another turning off to the left, ignore this and carry straight on. Your path slightly veers to the right and passes through a symmetrical avenue of conifers dropping you down to a stile. Following is a steep flight of steps, this being provided with a

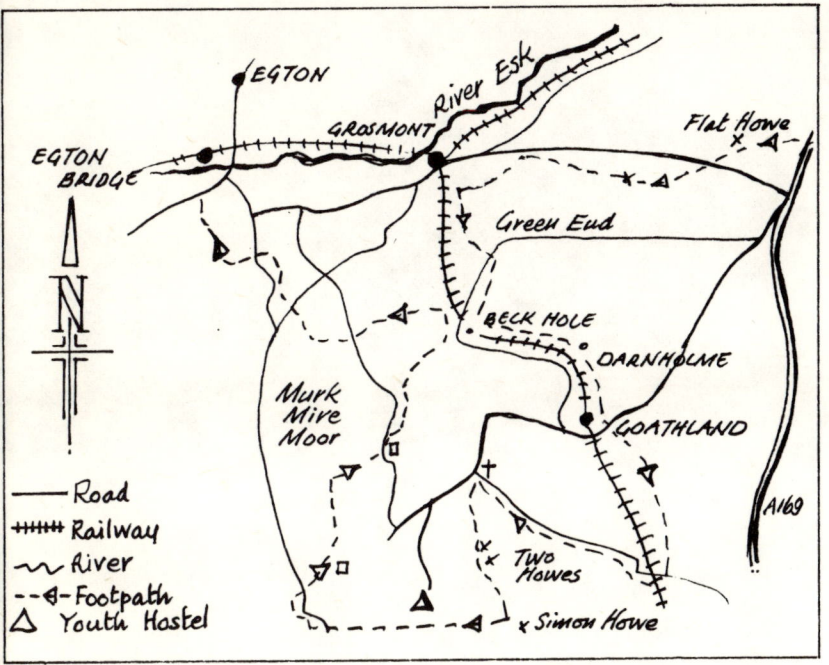

handrail for steadiness. A footbridge takes you over West Beck and after passing through a gate you arrive on to the old trackway of a discontinued railway line; Beckhole can be seen just beyond.

Turn left and in a short distance you will cross the Eller Beck by stepping stones. It is now very pleasurable and easy walking; 600 yards of walking will bring you to a left-hand turn. Looking down this track a gate will be seen across it and fixed to a bar of the gate a plaque showing the name, Egton. Turn down here passing through the gate and crossing Oakley Beck by a bridge of good breadth. A few more yards and a second footbridge is crossed being of narrower dimensions and, believe it or not, in a few more yards a third footbridge is crossed. On crossing, follow the path up the slope where it joins the main track which has forded the beck.

Turn left and follow this track which turns to the left and in front of the house known as Murkside. Just a little to the rear of this house the path divides. Take the right-hand path, a sign and way marker is of assistance. A field gate is stretched across your path but you can get through it easily. A fairly steep climb is now undertaken, but it is smooth grassy walking, most pleasant and extremely peaceful. Just prior to reaching the Egton road a couple of signs and way markers

give guidance to a step ladder stile which takes you over on to the road.

Turn left on the road and in a short distance you will pass the cottage, Struntry Carr. Just past the cottage a footpath sign directs you through a gate on to the moor. Follow the path keeping the wall on your right and after climbing for about 250 yards you pass through a wicket gate. on to Murk Mire Moor. The path is quite distinct at first but narrow as you come out on to the plateau top. Over on your left the Yorkshire Water Authority reservoir, Randy Mire, can be seen glistening through the trees. Over on your right a fine view can be seen of Whitby and the sea beyond.

You now come to a group of quite small ponds; they will be most probably dried up in the middle of a hot summer. Keep these ponds on your left and shortly you will pick up some vehicle tracks. Follow these; they twist and turn a little and at one stage it becomes a single track for a few yards and then it becomes a good track once more. The track shortly develops into a pleasant green sward which leads you to a metalled road. A six foot standing stone marks the junction of the path with the road. Cross the road and within 30 yards your path will bring you to another metalled road and a further standing stone. This road drops you down a 1 in 5 bank to Egton Bridge coming out near the *Horseshoe Inn*.

Follow this road passing through a gate and approximately within half a mile a farm track turns off to the left. Turn down here and where the track turns sharply to the left to Swang Farm, a branch track which appears to be little used turns off to the right. Turn down here and in 60 yards you come to a dead end. On the left a timber fence looks down a small field to Hall Grange Farm. There is no gate or stile, but it is a right-of-way. Climb over the fence, go down the field, it is steep and quite wet. Pass through the field gate with the farm on your right; this leads directly out on to a wide farm track. Turn right and follow it to the junction of the Egton Bridge/Rosedale road. This is a delightful area to walk in, no doubt you will be attracted to the bubbling Butter Beck near the road junction just as I was.

You have now walked a distance of 12½ miles and may be thinking of accommodation for the night. If you turn to the right a walk of about half a mile will bring you down to Egton Bridge. Since commencing the walk you have now covered a total distance of 27 miles.

3. Egton Bridge to Old Margery

IF you are to continue with the walk turn left up the road and shortly you will reach the junction with that popular footpath which comes through East Arncliff Woods. Just past here the road steepens considerably, and I am sorry to say that ahead is a 1 in 3 road climb to Delves. However, you have some consolation in the beauty of the views; it is very satisfying. Delves Cottage is of interest, being one of the few remaining thatched roof cottages in the area. I believe that it is quite old. I know a man who was brought up as a child in this cottate, a real dyed-in-the-wool dalesman. The road levels out slightly just past Delves, but there will be a mile of steady uphill walking before you arrive at a cattle grid. On your left is the moor and on your right the forestry.

Over the cattle grid the grass verge opens out into a wide grassy area which is a popular spot for picnickers. A path can be picked up here which takes you at an angle and then alongside the forest for 300 yards, this bringing you to a gate and a stile. Cross over the stile and follow the path through the forest which is quite wet and muddy. The path goes down at an angle eventually bringing you out into the valley of Glaisdale.

As you emerge from the forest, Glaisdale opens out before you. Fine views are obtained for the full length of the dale and up and across to Glaisdale Rigg. For a short distance your path curves to the left and follows the contour with a stone wall on your right. On coming to a field gate on your right, pass through and continue downhill, a further stone wall is on your right. On coming to the end of this stone wall your path veers to the left and a steep, rough, wet and muddy walk is undertaken to Bank House Farm; it is still fine walking. On coming to Bank House Farm pass through the field gate into the farm yard and continue to a broad farm track which leads to the road just above New House Farm. With reference to accommodation, 1½ to 2 miles will bring you to Glaisdale village and about 1 mile will bring you to Rock Head Farm.

To continue turn left along this road which leads updale. I have tried to keep road walking down to a minimum, but if all that is best is to be seen, sometimes there has been no alternative. One consolation is that it is an interesting road with not a great deal of traffic on it, even in summer.

We are now heading updale, passing High and Low Gill Farms and Nab End. The occupiers of Nab End have altered some farm buildings into holiday flatlets; they do not look out of place and

Glaisdale Head Farm.

appear to be in keeping with the rest of the dale. Mountain Ash Farm is passed as the road curves to the right. A fine walk of about a mile over the moor can be taken from off the Rosedale road down to Mountain Ash; remember this for another day. Hob Cottage with its mullioned windows is very attractive as it looks down the full length of the dale.

Just past Yew Grange Farm a single width road turns off to the left. Take this road; you will find that it climbs steeply for ¾ mile on to Glaisdale Moor and the Rosedale/Glaisdale Rigg road. On reaching this road make a halt to regain your breath and to soak in the fine view looking down the Glaisdale valley. Turn right on this road and follow it for nearly half a mile to where the bridlepath turns off on the left to Trough House. This path is signposted.

Take the bridlepath to Trough House; you are now back on the Coast to Coast route but not for long. A good mile of moor walking is now undertaken as we traverse round Great Fryup Head. This is a wild moor, with rough wiry heather, a moor that stirs the heart, especially if you walk it in winter with a keen biting wind blowing round you, or the ground frozen hard with frost. It puts colour into your cheeks, gives you a hearty appetite, and you certainly do not require any sleeping pills for that night.

On coming to a cairn a path will be seen turning off on your right and heading for the drop down into Great Fryup Dale. Before making the descent, stop and have a good long look at this most spectacular view over one of the most beautiful parts of the north of

23

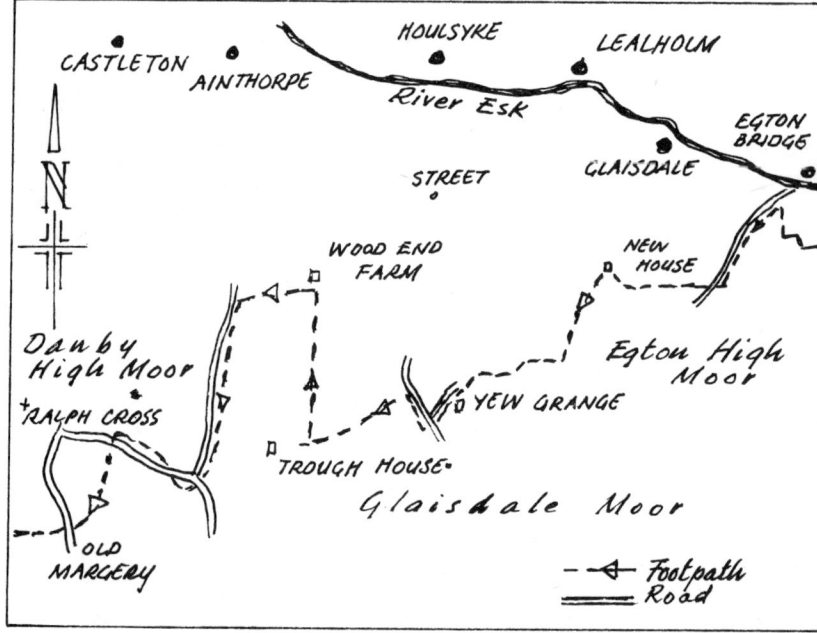

England; the two Fryups, Little and Great, are divided by that fine ridge which rises up from Fairy Cross Plain. Fine walking is to be had on this ridge.

You now take leave of the Coast to Coast route as you begin to descend the face of Great Fryup Head; the path zig-zags a little as it is quite precipitous. On reaching the bottom the way undulates a little and you cross a small beck. Head for a field gate in a stone wall which crosses your path. As you pass between this wall a new metal-clad hut will be seen a little to your left. The path can be seen veering over to the left as it wends its way on to the moor. Shortly you will pick up a stone wall on your right; this wall and continuing walls and fences is your guide to Wood End Farm. After a while you drop into and then immediately out of a steep dip. You then pass into another pasture through an opening in a stone wall. The stone wall continues on your right but this gives way to a wire fence.

On coming to the nest field gate you pass out on to the moor of bracken and within 30 yards you are back into another pasture. Your path now lies within a hollow with the remnants of a stone wall on your left, this eventually giving way to a patchy hedge. The next field gate brings you into a further pasture, the hedge is now on your right. One more pasture and the path leads out on to the metalled road just to the left of Wood End Farm. Turn left along this road.

24

Just prior to Slydney Beck Farm, map reference, NZ 720038, a right-of-way crosses the field on your left and follows the stone wall on your left. At the top of this field you enter a walled lane just to the left of Woodhead Farm. On arriving at Woodhead Farm turn left into a further walled lane. At the end of the lane pass through a field gate into a pasture. Keeping the stone wall on your left you pass through a further field gate on to the moor. A ruined barn will be seen just up on your right; passing this barn your path is picked up easily as it zig-zags its way up to the intake wall. This is fine walking in this most beautiful area of the North York Moors. I am never happier than when out walking in countryside of this nature.

On passing through a gate leading on to the moor, a good track will be seen a little over to the right — don't be tempted, this is not your path. Look for a faint path at nearly half left and in about a hundred yards of climbing you will come to three very large stones. A long straight depression leads straight ahead in your direction of walking. Where this depression begins to fade out look to your left and the path can be picked up again. After a short distance a small cairn will be seen, the road is only 20 yards ahead of this cairn. You come across the road suddenly as it lays in a slight depression below the heather.

On reaching the road turn left and 1½ miles will bring you to the Rosedale/Castleton road. This road was first tar sprayed in 1932 and no doubt it would not be much better than a good track before this time. I can imagine that the stone knapper would spend all his working day breaking stones for in-filling of pot holes. Turn right on this road and in just over ¼ mile of walking the Lyke Wake Walk path will be seen to cross the road. You have the choice of joining the Lyke Wake path which can be quite wet and muddy in parts, or going by the road.

Either way, on reaching Fat Betty (the Ordnance map shows her as White Cross), a signpost on the left of the road points in the direction over the moor to the Hutton-le-Hole road. This path is still part of the Lyke Wake Walk and is quite pleasant walking. It can be picked out quite easily these days after the tramp of thousands of feet, but this was not always the case a few years ago.

Since leaving Butter Beck at its point of contact with the Egton Bridge road, you have travelled about 12¼ miles and no doubt you will be thinking of accommodation. On arriving at the Hutton-le-Hole road, straight across will be seen a good track guarded by a large flat standing stone, known as Old Margery. From Old Margery you will have a walk of three to four miles to Danby Dale or Castleton or, by carrying on, 3½ miles to the Westerdale Youth Hostel. You have now walked a total of 39½ miles since leaving Whitby, plus whatever mileage has been covered in obtaining accommodation.

4. Old Margery to Kildale

SAY goodbye to Old Margery and then step out along the track; a few old shooting butts will keep you company for part of the way. This path leads to Esklets and upper Westerdale — there is some great walking ahead. It is fairly level going for a while and then, as you cross between the remnants of an old intake wall, the path steepens and becomes much rougher. The dale begins to open up before you and fine extensive views are beheld. I think that Westerdale is one of the finest dales in the whole of the North York Moors and you are now about to enter on a part of the walk which is of great moorland beauty.

The path can be seen quite clearly and it takes you between two giant gate stoups, then veers to the right. The way is now marked by a series of short posts with white-painted tops and leads over to a stone wall. Follow this wall down to the corner where another white-topped post denotes where you turn right passing through a gate in the wall. Keep walking down dale with the stone wall on your left and very shortly you will come to a very good track which climbs. After only 50 yards' walking you come out into the open once more and another white-topped stake is seen just in front of you. Looking straight ahead, a very good broad track can be seen crossing your path; make for this and then turn right.

The Lyke Wake Walk has now been left for good so let us press on and concentrate on the Eskdale Way. After crossing a small beck you then follow the track between stone walls which shortly opens out into a small paddock. Near the top right-hand corner is a large heap of rubble, stones and broken tiles; this is the remains of Esklets. It is sad to see it in this state having known it when it had a roof on.

Follow the path by the rubble into the top corner where a new stile (at the time of writing) is negotiated. Follow the stone wall on your left through a pasture and then the path becomes defined once more and easy to follow. Cross over a stile and your path leads you down to the infant Esk which is crossed by a footbridge. Follow the footpath for about ¾ mile or just over to where the way divides near to a standing stone. Turn left, this bringing you down to the Esk and a field gate. Pass through keeping the fence on your left. Cross over another stile into a second pasture and then pass through a broken wall; the way has now become very muddy.

On approaching a good farm track, this coming down from Waites Farm, a water splash and a footbridge are to be seen on your left. Cross the footbridge and turn right as indicated by a footpath sign.

Very shortly you come to another footbridge over a beck; cross this into a small pasture. Look for a stile which gives entry to Wood End, passing the rear of the farm to a field gate. Pass through turning left; at the end of this pasture cross another stile which takes you towards the farm track coming from Hill House.

Cross the track keeping the fence on your right, aiming for the right-hand corner of this field. Cross over another stile and then follow the overhead electric wires which brings you to a footbridge. Cross two more fields and then you come out onto a good farm track; New House (now not so new looking) is on your left. Turn right and follow this track for about ¾ mile. When you come almost opposite Grange Farm, the path climbs up to the left cutting the corner off and leading to a field gate about 50 yards up from the wall corner. Pass through the field gate and now keep the wall on your right. Three more fields and you come to Hawthorne House; don't pass through the farm yard, keep straight on after passing through the field gate. Cross two more pastures, finally passing through a gate on to a narrow metalled road on the moor.

This road climbs steeply at first and then levels out a little. In about 500 yards of walking a small cairn will be seen on the left-hand side of the road. This denotes the path to take over Little and Great Hograh Moors. You have now witnessed the delights of walking Westerdale and its surrounding moors and now, following on, the pleasures of the Hograh moors and Baysdale. Great country, great walking.

This path is well defined and climbs steadily up Little Hograh Moor; it is a little rough in parts but really fine moor walking. Quite a few large rocks and standing stones are to be seen protruding through the thick healthy-looking heather. Little Hograh Beck is crossed and in just over a mile of walking you drop down to a small but interesting old stone bridge which crosses Great Hograh Beck at the end of a large belt of trees. Just before you drop down to the bridge a stone memorial has been placed on a large flat rock and encased in a mound of stones in the form of a cairn. The inscription reads:

ALAN CLEGG
1936-1981
WHO LOVED THESE MOORS

The bridge makes a lovely spot in warm weather to call a halt and partake of refreshment whilst you behold the view. To carry on, go straight ahead up a short but very steep bank. On the path reaching the top of this bank it bears half left, crossing two sets of tracks made by Land Rover or farm tractors. Shortly afterwards the path inconveniently fades out, but if you walk parallel to a straightly aligned, narrow hollow for about 50 yards the path is picked up once more and then becomes quite easy to follow. About half a mile of walking brings you to a sharp pointed cairn on the top of a rise. On

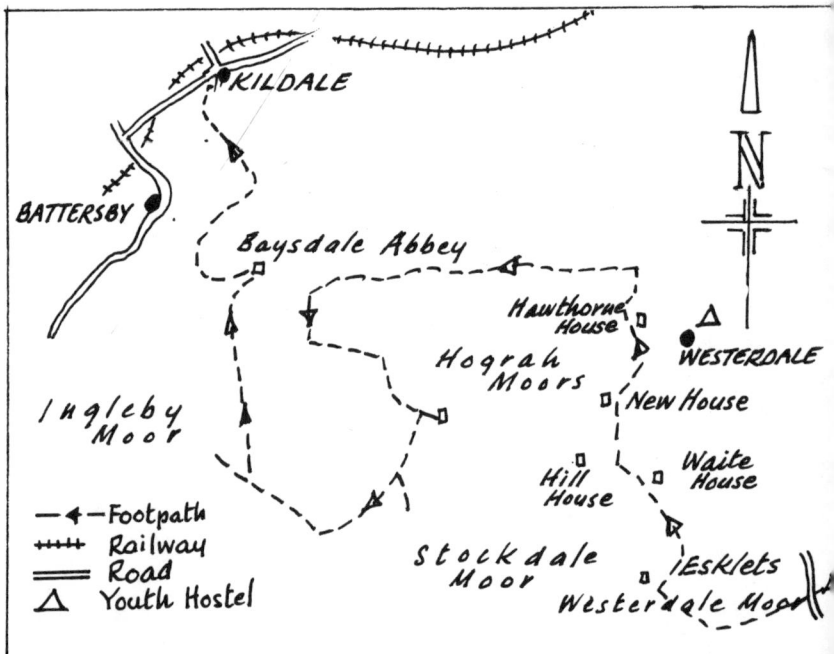

reaching this cairn fine views are to be seen over Baysdale. Cook's monument on Easby Moor is quite plain to see over and beyond Baysdale.

I have reconnoitred the next part of the walk and the rights-of-way shown on O.S. Pathfinder NZ.60/70 do not altogether line up with paths you find on the ground. If you follow the following directions I do not think that you will go far wrong. As you leave the cairn the path continues in a straight line for a short distance and then fades. If you aim for the corner of a stone wall, keeping this wall on your left you will pick up a path once more which leads to a gate at the junction of the wall with the forestry. Pass through this gate and follow the broad track with the forest on your right.

Shortly you will come to a gated track coming out of the forest which crosses your path. Turn left on this track and climb up the moor to the moor fence and another gate. Pass through and follow the track over the moor. This track is basically to facilitate travel to shooting butts and a shooting hut. After progressing for about ½ mile keep a sharp look-out for a track turning off on your right. As a guide, No. 5 shooting butt is the nearest to this turning off point and a small heap of stones indicates where to turn.

The path is quite good to follow for about ½ mile and then you divert along a narrow path on your right. A guide is that about 10 yards from the diversion is a heap of large stones, probably a broken down cairn. Just as you turn a directional arrow of small stones and a further small heap of stones indicates your way. About a mile of walking will bring you down a drop to Armouth Wath. It is fine wild moorland scenery here. A broken down sheep fold nestles between the confluence of two small becks. Both becks are bridged by miniature stone bridges.

Having crossed the two becks you begin to climb steeply; it is very wet and reedy, typical slack terrain. On the path levelling out a little the way becomes drier and walking improves greatly. About ½ mile distant from the sheep fold you come to a track branching off to the left which leads over Ingleby Moor; ignore this path and just keep straight on. As you come down to the lower reaches the rough moor changes to short velvety grasses reminiscent of the grasses in the Craven country of the Pennines. On coming to a stone wall, pass through the gate and follow the path to a small thinly-planted coniferous plantation. Your path twists through this plantation for a short distance and on emerging you pass through a gate alongside a broken stile.

I recall on one occasion when I was walking in the opposite direction towards this gate that I saw a stoat which appeared to be twisting or cavorting about. A few yards away four or five pheasants were stood and they seemed to be unaware of the stoat's presence. On my footsteps being heard, up flew the pheasants and the stoat fled for a crevice in the stone wall. On approaching the wall the stoat was there peering out at me and then like a flash he or she was gone. I have read or heard from somewhere that a stoat will put on an act to arouse the curiosity of its intended victim and then pounce at the right moment. My only thought on this is that you would think a pheasant would be too big and heavy for a stoat to hold down. I recall my father telling the story that he once saw a stoat grab hold of a crow. Immediately the crow took off into the air, the stoat hung on for a short time and then thought better of it and dropped to the ground.

The track can be seen twisting down this quite steep slope to a gap between a stone wall and a wire fence. Pass through this gap and head for the white field gate which comes out on to the road just to the left of the farm, Baysdale Abbey.

This farm is built on the site of a Cistercian nunnery. No doubt much of the stonework of the present day farm came from the Abbey church and other monastic buildings some time after the dissolution. Little is known of the old abbey except that it was founded somewhere about the end of the 12th century by nuns of the Cistercian order and that they came from Thorpe, known today as Nunthorpe. There is a record available of a survey which was carried out of the abbey buildings at or about the time of the dissolution and gives an idea of size, construction, and uses. The church was built of stone and measured 65 ft. x 20 ft. A further range of buildings measuring 50 ft. x 16 ft. which included the frater and other chambers, was described as having walls of timber and a roof of slate and thatch. In those days it would be a quiet, peaceful place in summer, but very difficult to get out of in the heart of winter.

On leaving Baysdale Abbey turn left and follow the metalled road leading out of the dale. The road climbs steeply and twists up past Abbey Farm. On reaching the top where the road turns sharply to the right, a broad track which is the route of the Cleveland Way joins you from the left. It is about 2½ miles from Baysdale Abbey along this road to the junction with the main Kildale road, but you have fine extensive views over towards Hasty Bank, the Vale of Mowbray and the Pennines some twenty odd miles beyond.

On joining the main road turn right and within five minutes you will be in Kildale village. You have now walked a total of 13½ miles since leaving Old Margery and may be thinking of accommodation in Kildale. Your total mileage from the beginning of the walk now stands at 52¾ miles.

5. Kildale to Danby

IT would be wrong at this stage not to include a few words about one of Kildale's residents, Roland Close, now passed on. Roland Close was a typical country estate worker, an ordinary man, who would not have wished it otherwise. His life long interest was in archaeology, spending many hours of his spare time in searching, digging, sorting and recording his finds on these moors. Iron and Bronze Age artifacts are among his collection, some of which no doubt many museums would like to have. Probably his most interesting discovery was the base stones of three Brigantian huts on Percy Rigg. These are now fenced off and a memorial plaque is displayed; he died in 1981. His knowledge was very extensive and academic experts of archaeology would consult him as to his opinions on this subject. Kildale should be very proud of one of its sons.

Follow the metalled road passing Bankside Farm and Cottage. The road begins to steepen as you become enfolded in extensive forestry. As you emerge from the forest Lounsdale Farm can be seen below. An unusual name is Lounsdale; it is probably derived from the old dialect word *Lounn,* a 'loun place' being a sheltered place. I imagine that Lonsdale is a variation of the same word. On passing Lounsdale Farm keep straight on; passing through a field gate you begin to climb till you reach Lounsdale Plantation.

Here you can have a choice of routes. You can take the steep climb through the forest to the road at the top of Percy Rigg and then turn right, walking down the road to the farm track junction to Sleddale Farm. If you take this route you will pass the base stones of Roland Close's Brigantian huts. The alternative and pleasanter route is to follow the broad track on your right which shortly enters the plantation. On coming to a Y-junction, take the left-hand fork; it begins to steepen and is muddy and rough in places but press on. You do not walk far before you come to a T-junction; here you turn to the left and within 200 yards you are in daylight once more and on to the road.

Turn left on the road and in a very short distance you come to the farm road on your right leading to Sleddale Farm. It is very pleasant walking as you follow the Sleddale Farm track — it dips and twists as it crosses the Sleddale Beck. Just after you have passed the Sleddale Farm gate, a path is seen to turn off to the left. This is the one that you want; climbing it makes its way along the flanks of a fairly high ridge. As you climb so the views improve. Follow the general direction of this path and it brings you to the corner of Guisborough Woods, just a little north of east of Cod Farm (also known as Highcliff Farm).

A small gate is seen at this corner of the wood, and now for a change you will follow the Cleveland Way for a short distance. Follow the path for about 200 yards alongside the edge of the wood and when you come to a gate on your left a path will be seen to turn off to the right and enter the wood. In only a short distance a broad forestry road will be crossed, your path rising steeply back into the trees. You will find this part of the route marked with way markers and the Cleveland Way sign. In a very short time you will find yourself out at the foot of Highcliff Nab. Take the steep path to the right of the Nab and climb up to the top. Here you will want to regain your breath and no better place could be found. What a delightful panoramic view overlooking the town of Guisborough and across to Eston Moor.

After you have absorbed the view and are ready for off once more, carry on along this ridge path which follows the contour and in a short distance it re-enters the forest and joins a broad forest drive. It is easy and pleasant walking through this wood which is well patronised by the local population of Guisborough and district as well as long distance walkers. On coming to a Y-junction take the right hand branch; after walking for a ¼ mile you will come to a cross track. Turn right and you will be able to see the gate which takes you onto the moor. On coming out of the wood, keep straight on across Guisborough Moor; you will have little difficulty with this crossing to the Commondale road. You will see a post sticking up out of the top of a cairn — an arrow mark on the post points in the direction of your path.

You will come to a broad track which is for vehicular access to shooting butts; go straight across, the path is well defined. After travelling for about ½ mile, if you look over to the left on the top of the ridge you will see a number of standing stones and tumuli — this is known as Hob on the Hill. A number of writers of local history have made reference to the hobs who populated these parts more than a century ago and well beyond, and the influence that these hobs had on the lives of the local community. A memorial stone is passed and is of interest. It commemorates the deaths of two guardsmen who died through action in the first world war. They were both volunteers, one of whom shepherded his father's flocks on these moors. The Hon. Margaret Bruce Chaloner thought it most fitting that a memorial should be erected to these two lads who spent so much of their time on the moors. Most of the farms in the Commondale parish belonged to the Chaloner estates. Joseph Ford, a stone mason who lived the latter part of his life in Castleton, was engaged to engrave and erect the memorial at this spot.

A little beyond the memorial is a green-painted hut used by shooting parties. A short way beyond the hut the path divides, the left-hand path crossing over a timber bridge; this is the path you take. A further ¼ mile and the path forks once more. Take the right-hand

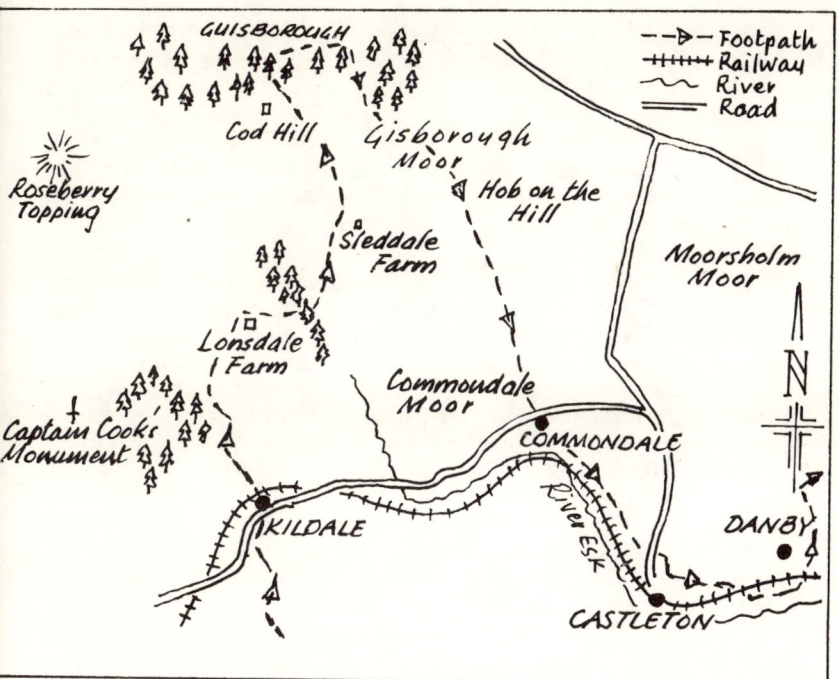

fork this time; a post with a directional arrow marks the spot. Two or three hundred yards further and you come to a cairn. Take the path which bears to the right of this cairn; it heads down to a small runnel which has to be crossed. If you aim towards the largest of a number of quite small trees, it has a broken limb which is bent over; the crossing of the runnel is just to the left of this tree. You will not have any more difficulties; having crossed the runnel you now begin to climb by way of a paved trod. This eventually runs out but your path joins the farm road from North Ings just beyond a gate. Follow the farm road and in a few short yards you will arrive at the road, on the other side of which is a green area used for car parking.

You now have two choices of route once more. No doubt if you require a shop, cafe or inn you turn left and head down the road for Commondale village. Commondale as a community has been there a long time; in the 12th century it was recorded and known as Colmondale. In the year 1753 a bleach mill was built, the site being on Commondale Beck two or three hundred yards from the present day railway station, or should I say halt. Most of the farms in these dales carried out a cottage industry of weaving a cloth for the making of clothes. On completion the finished cloth required bleaching and so it was sent from far and wide to the bleach mill here in

Commondale. Later in the 19th century a brickyard was built and appeared to be quite successful. Later still the pottery industry was established and finally during the first world war the clay works were utilised in the manufacture of poison gas. The poison gas was stored in bulk at the Skinningrove Iron and Steel works and was therefore the principal reason for the Zeppelin air attacks on the works at that time. I recall that my father who was living quite close to the works at that time said they made five visitations but little or no damage or casualties resulted.

If you do not require to go into Commondale, cross the road and aim centrally across the green area and you will come to a field gate. Pass through this field gate into a pasture and walk straight ahead keeping the stone wall on your right. Pass through a second pasture and then enter a lane near two or three houses. At the end of the lane where it joins the road turn left; within 200 yards a turning will be seen to the right in front of a farm. A signpost points the way to Commondale railway station. Take this lane and follow it round the white cement-faced bungalow. The track is easy to follow as it undulates its way through pastures, a small plantation and bracken moor. You cross a couple of singing becks and you can look down on to the Esk Valley railway line and Commondale Beck. It is most beautiful here and I find it most satisfying.

On coming out on to the road a decision has to be made as to whether you require shops, cafe, bar meals or accommodation. If so it is a steep drop and then a steep climb up to Castleton's main street. Otherwise you can continue the walk which approximates to the same contour on the opposite side of the road, and have the pleasure of the views looking down and across the valley and looking up Danby Dale.

Turn down the road in the Castleton direction and within 150 yards you will come to a track turning off to the left, named Sunny Brow. Good walking is now to be had all the way to Danby. Your path takes you through Danby Park, a fairly large plantation of silver birch, these being sprinkled with a few other deciduous varieties of tree. After leaving the plantation your path shortly begins to drop away towards the Danby road. On arriving at the road a distance of not much more than ¼ mile will bring you to the crossroads near the *Duke of Wellington Inn*. Your day's walking now totals 11¾ miles and your sum total 64½ miles.

6. Danby to Whitby

CROSS the road to the *Duke of Wellington* and then continue along the road to Lealholm. After about 100 yards of walking you will see a row of terraced cottages on your left. At the end of this terrace turn up to the left on to the green and on coming to the stone wall on your left turn right and follow the path which leads on to the moor. On coming to the end of the wall your path continues straight ahead. Shortly you will come to an angled wall on your right. Here you take the track bearing away slightly to the left. In a short while you will see the farm ahead known as Doubting Castle; this you will circumnavigate in due course.

On your path reaching the road, turn right and in a hundred yards take the farm track on the right — this leads to Doubting Castle. Keep following the wire fence which turns in an arc; keep straight on. On coming to the end of the fence the path divides. You can take the slightly shorter route to the left which takes you across the moor to the Danby Beacon road, or the path to the right which is more picturesque, taking you by the Clither Beck. Your path goes downhill at an angle and at times can be a bit wet and muddy. Near to the bottom of the slope you come to the beck; here a step ladder stile, built for giants, takes you over a wall and you are now in the wood. A few short yards and you cross the beck by a footbridge.

I find this spot very enchanting, it giving me much pleasure on the many times that I have walked through it. It was here that one winter's day I saw a stoat in its full winter coat of ermine. The trees are mainly the typical English oak, ash and alder, but with the sun shining through casting its beams of glancing light on to the singing, tumbling beck it is a place which makes you want to linger. What an unusual name this beck has. Canon Atkinson states that this name is of Scandinavian origin. The Icelandic language of today is the nearest of the modern Scandinavian languages to Old Scandinavian, in other words the language of the Danes and Vikings. The Icelandic ar-klior means the clattering or murmuring sound of a stream. It can be seen that after the passage of time the name has gradually changed to Clither.

Your path now comes out of the wood and passes through a gap in a wall, then turns left, crosses a stile and then back over the beck via a footbridge. The path now takes quite a wet and stiff climb, veering over to a stone wall on your right. Now follow the stone wall as it curves round to the right finally leaving it as your path joins the road to Danby Beacon. Turn left and follow this road, climbing just about ¾ mile to the beacon.

Joseph Ford, the same man who carved the monument on Commondale Moor had a friend in his young days who was then an old man. This friend stated that his father knew quite well the soldier and his wife who lived in a stone-built dwelling on Danby Beacon. Their job was to light the beacon if and when the invasion forces of Napoleon were sighted. No doubt our forefathers of that time were quite pleased that this duty was never carried out. Danby Beacon was the first inland beacon from the coast.

Do you remember those fine vistas from Fryup Head and when you walked by Woodhead and Woodend Farms? If you now look towards the dales of Little and Great Fryup you will see the views from the opposite angle and no doubt you will agree that they are no less exciting for a change of position. On a warm day you can sit and the time will slip by you as you take in this great expanse of moorland ridges and their luxuriant verdant valleys. If you look to the south-west to the near left of Danby Rigg, you may be able to discern Danby Castle, now a working farm. Closer observation will show that there are still elements of its construction which indicate that it is part of a fortified castle. No doubt all the stone work of the farm outbuildings will be the re-used stone of the original castle.

Now well rested we must carry on taking the broad track eastwards; it is mainly a gradual descent and the walking is easy. Good views are obtained as you travel for about 1¼ miles to a Y-junction. Take the right-hand track and within 300 yards you will join the Oakley Walls metalled road. A further quarter of a mile of walking and you join the Stonegate/Lealholm road. Turn right and a steep walk downhill will take you into Lealholm. As you pass the road junction with Lealholmside you will note a large rock on the green. A small plaque is attached which commemorates the death of two United States Airforce officers on 27th April, 1979, when their jet fighter crashed, ploughing across the fields and breaking through stone walls in its travel. Miraculously no civilians or houses were involved. The commemoration was by subscription by the residents of Lealholm.

Now down in this picturesque village of Lealholm, you will find toilets, two tea rooms at time of writing, shop and the *Board Inn* which provides bed and breakfast.

On leaving Lealholm take the farm track that turns off to the left just past the car park; this will soon bring you alongside the river which meanders up to the farm named Underpark. Follow the track round to the right of the farm buildings, passing through a field gate into a pasture. Your path now narrows and follows the river more closely. On arriving at the end of this pasture a stile will be seen through the trees. Cross this stile, then a footbridge and in a few yards you will come out and join the broad track coming from Lealholmside. Now turn right and you will shortly see in front of you

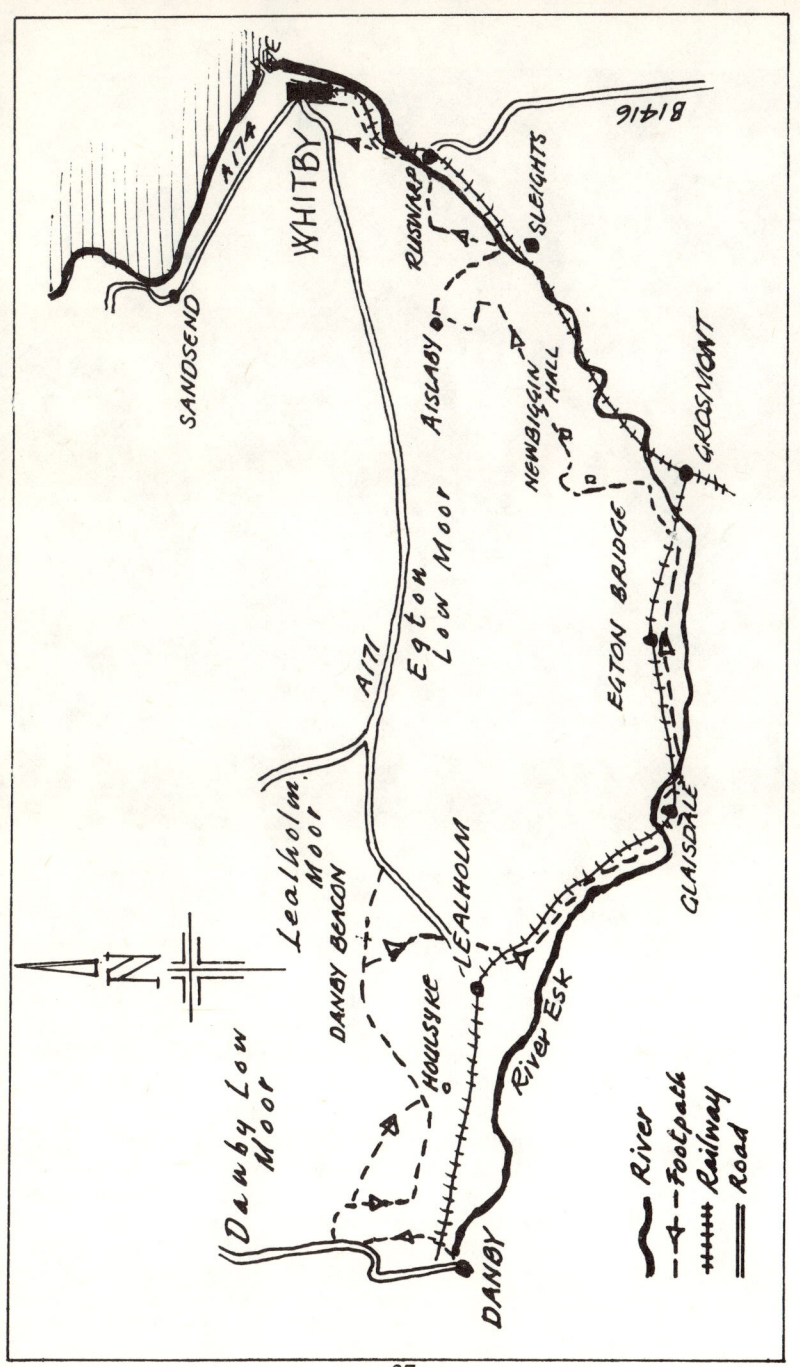

Danby Castle, the ruined stronghold on the south side of the Esk Valley.

the railway bridge which crosses the river. On approaching the bridge your path turns sharply to the right and crosses the river by a footbridge. The track curves and then rises steeply to a cottage on your left. Just past the cottage your track joins a metalled road; turn right and keep straight on till you reach the cottage at Thorneywaite. If you wish to go to the higher part of Glaisdale village, go straight ahead; it will bring you out at the Green. Post office, general store, butchers and the *Mitre Inn* are all available at this end of the village.

To carry on with the walk, pass between the first and second houses, a signpost marks the spot, then cross a stile into a pasture. A second pasture is crossed and then a third stile gives entry into the edge of Miller's Wood. The path is straight forward and so gives you opportunity to take in the best of this countryside. The River Esk is exceptionally fine at this point as it tumbles over a rock-strewn bed, it is most idyllic and well worth seeing.

38

On coming to a delightful cottage beside the river the path broadens out and then rises steeply out of the wood and on to the road that leads to Anglers' Quarters. Turn left on this road which you will find quite steep and twisting. Your consolation for having to walk on the road is that it is downhill and the houses and cottages flanking are quite interesting. As you pass down this road, the long row of terraced cottages to the right are known as Anglers' Quarters. I have enquired but have had no success in trying to find the reason or origin of this unusual name. Your road shortly joins the main road opposite the *Arncliff Arms* — residential, bar meals available.

Here we turn left and wend our way down to the Beggars Bridge. As you drop down it is useful to observe the toilets at the entrance to the railway station. Now you are down at Beggars Bridge, an interesting and popular spot, a rendezvous point of cars and people.

I am now going to take you up Limber Hill, a 1 in 3 climb. You may well ask why go up a steep road like that with a passable amount of traffic on it in the height of summer, when you have the lovely Arncliff Woods on the spot. Yes the Armcliff Woods are well worth walking through, but as compensation for your hard slog up Limber, I will take you through fields and a wood which are a pleasure to cross and which may not be known to some of you.

On reaching the top of the bank you will see Limber Hill Farm; turn through the farm yard, technically it should be the second opening and take the right-hand of the two gates, following the track across the field. The TV booster mast will be seen over on your right in this field. Cross the next stile (it is way marked) and keep the hedge on your right. Your path brings you to another stile giving entry into a wood; the path now drops very steeply. A further stile brings you out of the wood into another pasture; cross this pasture slightly to the left and it will bring you down to a very small beck which is crossed by a broad plank bridge. On crossing turn right keeping the fence and the wood on your right. On coming to the stile you cross out on to the Egton Bridge road.

Turn right down this road and just over a ¼ mile of walking will bring you into the centre of the village. Egton Bridge is one of the prettiest of villages in the whole of the North of England. Set in the bottom of the valley it is surrounded by a multitude of large trees, the river looking its best as it turns and rushes over its rock-strewn bed. What more peaceful rural scene could you wish to see than an angler in thigh-high waders throwing his line in search of trout or salmon? In summer it is very popular with visitors and therefore you may have to run the gauntlet with passing traffic.

If you have the time it will be well worth your while to pause here and have a look at what Egton Bridge has to offer. Its most exalted son is no doubt Nicholas Postgate, usually known as Father Postgate, who was born in Egton Bridge. If you turn right and cross over the road bridge which spans the Esk, you will see on the left in about forty yards a gate which gives access to a track leading to two houses. The first is a long bungalow type of dwelling and it is thought that the older cottage known as Kirkdale House stood in very close proximity to this present day cottage. This was the reputed birthplace of Father Postgate in or about the year 1600.

Whilst in Egton Bridge do take time to have a look at St. Hedda's Church; it is in my opinion magnificent. Commencing in the west end of the south aisle, is a series of sculptures inset into the walls depicting the story leading up to the death of Christ. On the outside of the wall of the south aisle are also a series of paintings in pastel colours which are well worth looking at. Egton Bridge can provide you with a post office but no shop. The *Horse Shoe Inn* is residential, has a restaurant and bar meals are provided. *The Postgate* also provides bar meals and I believe is residential.

When you have seen all that you want to see in Egton Bridge your mind will once more return to walking. To continue, almost opposite St. Hedda's church will be seen a wide gate opening, the sides of which have white-painted fencing, and a notice indicates that it is the road to Egton Estates Office. Take this track which is an old toll road to Grosmont. You will find it flat easy walking and most pleasant. On reaching the old toll house you will see a board affixed to the wall giving the toll payable for different kinds of traffic. It will be noted that the board is comparatively modern even if the charges belie its age. It was first exhibited by the Egton Estates in 1948.

On reaching the main road, turn right for Grosmont if you want accommodation, shop or cafe. If you wish to carry on, turn left. Within 40 yards you will come to a road junction on the right — turn down here. On one occasion I saw a dipper flying in and out of the culvert which takes a small beck under the road at this particular spot. Continue down this road; it shortly winds round the small estate known as Priory Park. A short distance past this housing estate the road turns sharply to the left. A gate lies just in front of you giving access to a farm track which leads to Grosmont Farm. Over on your right is a fairly large stone house; this house lies adjacent to the site of the old Grosmont Priory, the remains of which are now non-existant.

Follow the farm track down to Grosmont Farm, passing through the farm yard which can be covered with slushy mud.. Carry on along this track to the next farm, Fotherley. On reaching Fotherley take the small gate on the left of the farm and, climbing, follow the paved trod through the wood. On arriving at the edge of the wood you pass into a field; crossing a stile, keep the edge of the wood on your right. From Fotherley Farm to the private road in Woodlands you will find the route quite well way marked and should not have any problems. On coming to the end of this field look for a wicket gate and stile about 50

Houlsyke, an Eskdale hamlet.

yards to your left. Cross over and follow the paved path to the metalled road.

Turn right and follow this road to Newbiggin Hall. As you will see by the appearance of the stonework, it is quite old. Apparently Newbiggin was a small dependent manor within the parish of Egton and belonged to the De Mauleys, Lords of Mulgrave. Along with other possessions this manor descended to the Salvin family by marriage. George Salvin married Elizabeth de Mauley in the year 1416, she being the aunt and joint heir of Peter de Mauley, the 8th Lord of Mulgrave. As they were without issue the manor stayed with the Salvin family for generations, certainly till towards the end of the 18th century. Originally there was a fortified house or small castle with a moat. This lay in ruins for a long period of time and then on the site was built a new house. The present house which you see is a further new building, the main part being built in the 16th century, the two wings being added at a later date.

You now go in front of Newbiggin Hall and its farm outbuildings, shortly passing through a field gate. You then pass through a number of pastures via wicket gates or stiles, skirting the edge of Hecks Wood. Whilst in this area it is of interest to look out sharply on your right-hand side for a gate stoup which is different to what you normally see. It is surprising but field gates have not been with us for such a long time, probably 200 years at the very most and possibly much less than that. What they used to use was a number of bars or poles, five or six in number, these being placed in equidistant holes in one gate stoup and the other ends of these poles being dropped into inverted L-shaped slots cut into the second gate stoup. These poles had to be removed and then replaced every time someone wished to pass through. I believe that there are quite a few of these old stoups scattered about this North York Moors area, but this is the only one that I can commit to memory. I would admit that it is more easily spotted when walking in the opposite direction.

Another couple of fields are crossed and then your track drops steeply through a small wood. It is rough and very muddy and at the time of writing quite a deal of tree-felling and trimming is going on. The brashings add to the roughness of walking. The way bears a little to the right and comes to a metalled farm road through a wicket gate. Cross the road and follow the path down through some small trees and bushes. In about 25 yards, look on your left for a flight of stone steps which leads down to a footbridge across a beck. Pass through a gate and then follow the paved trod over the next pasture.

Now cross over a short piece of ground which has a liberal sprinkling of small trees and then pass through a field gate into a further pasture. Two pastures in all and then you come to a metalled farm road just below Lodge Farm. Turn right along this road and in about a 100 yards you will pass through a gate on your right just below Thistle Grove Farm. Thistle Grove reminds me of a man, now passed on, who told me that as a child he was travelling by horse and dray which was loaded with household furniture as his family was moving house. The date of this removal is known exactly, 16th December, 1914. As they were travelling along the road from Eskdaleside to Grosmont the shelling of Whitby began by the German battle cruiser *Derflinger*. Some of the shells were directed at the Coast Guard station, missed, and three of them struck Whitby Abbey, destroying a gateway and severely damaging the west wall of the nave. Frank said that as they travelled along the road on that particular day, a shell exploded in front of Thistle Grove Farm. This was the furthest distance inland that a shell exploded in the bombardment.

At the end of the farmyard precincts the path aims, slightly rising, to the top right hand corner of this field. Pass through a gate and then make your way straight up the field to the private road at Woodlands. Turn left up this road and after a short distance you pass through a side gate alongside the main gate which crosses the road. Thirty more yards and the track divides; take the right-hand one and climb up to the main street of Aislaby. This track is a bit steep, but there are parts where a halt may be taken to regain your breath and take in the extensive panoramic views. Aislaby is normally a quiet village with a number of interesting old houses, a church, post office and the *New Tavern* — bar snacks and bed and breakfast is available.

Turning right you walk to the end of the village where the main road turns at a right-angle to the left. Straight ahead is Featherbed Lane (a sign is displayed on the wall). At this point you have the choice of two routes; both routes run in parallel a field in distance apart. The easiest is to cross the stile near the footpath sign, walking between the two buildings. Cross a further stile into the field and walk straight ahead. The entry into the next field is quite ingenious. As there is a steep drop a fine, broad, strong-built step ladder is available to take you down to the stile. On crossing this stile, head over to the far left-hand corner where a further stile is crossed. In quick succession another stile on the left takes you on to a path between some fairly tall bushes. It drops steeply, ultimately taking you down some steps to come out at the junction of the private road to Woodlands. Cross over the main road and take the road signposted to Ruswarp. Two hundred yards along this road will bring you to a bus stop and just beyond you turn left up Carr Hill Lane.

Your alternative route is to carry on down Featherbed Lane; the paved way high up near the wall acts as a footpath. In about 100 yards a narrow enclosed lane turns off to the right; your paved way turns with it and continues down to the bottom where it makes its exit on to the main road. About half way down a bench seat will be seen where you can take a rest. A fine extensive view is beheld looking over to

Blue Bank and the wild rolling moors beyond. Take your time and take it in, you have travelled quite some distance now and have seen some wonderful scenery of varied nature. Only a few short miles remain before you are at the end of your walk. It is still good interesting walking, but make the best of what is left.

This path at the time of writing had been recently cleared and a first class job has been made of it. In fact it is the best that I have seen it in the last ten years. If the weather has been wet the paved stones can be quite slippy and quite a deal of care is required.

On arriving at the main road, turn right and walk down to the road junction to Ruswarp; the route is now the same as if you had used the first of these alternatives.

Continue up Carr Hill Lane; it is residential but the houses and bungalows are of many and varied designs, these being set amongst a large variety of trees of all sizes. I think that this lane is pleasanter walking than taking the main road which is parallel. On reaching the point where the lane turns to the left, a cul-de-sac of new houses turns off to the right, known as Ridge Lane. Turn down here and on reaching the end of this road turn left and take the field gate ahead.

On entering this field continue with the hedge on your right-hand side. It is usually sticky soil along this field but it is of flat terrain and fine views can be seen looking down to the Carrs and the line of the River Esk. On reaching the end of this field turn up with the hedge to the left and within 70 yards you will come to a stile. Keep straight ahead after crossing the stile, still keeping the hedge on your right until you pass through a field gate into an irregular shaped pasture. Keep to the left; with the hedge now on your left, you will see Lumbert Hill Farm over to the right. You are not long before you begin to drop down a bit of rough ground to a stile.

Now that you are over the stile you will find that you are on a small golf course; beware of flying golf balls! As you cross the golf course a tea room will come into sight; it is situated near the main gates down by the road — make for this point. Another larger cafe will be found across the road so you will not be hard put to in respect of refreshments. If you so wish you can take a boat and relax on the river. This is a very popular spot with motorists in the summer.

Turn to the left and walk towards Ruswarp passing Ruswarp Mill on the way. In the main the mill is quite an old building, being built by the engineer Philip Williams in 1752. This enterprise was financed by Nathaniel Chomley, a member of the well-known Chomley family who were Lords of the Manor of Whitby. This was not the first mill to be built at Ruswarp; records show that there was a corn mill here in the 13th century. The mill today has changed over from corn grinding to the processing of animal feed.

On reaching the T-junction, turn left and within 200 yards on the right-hand side of the road you will see a narrow ginnel running up the side of the Old Hall. Take this path which continues as a paved path through the fields after leaving the houses. On coming to a plantation the path steepens and a flight of steps have been laid to give assistance. Near the top a wicket gate gives access to a path which takes you to the top of Prospect Hill (A171) in Whitby; our path carries straight on. On coming to a kissing gate, pass through and cross the old discontinued railway track which is in a cutting by a footbridge. Through another gate, cross a small pasture and then another gate takes you across another discontinued railway track. Straight ahead will be seen school playing fields and your path goes straight across the centre of these fields and then alongside the school. This path is fenced in with timber on both sides.

On reaching Airey Hill Farm your path turns to the left through a small gate and at the present time comes out on to the entrance of the school. Go down this school road to join the main road. Cross the road, over the stile and then continue following the path over a rough pasture. Shortly the path drops steeply to the road, but it is worth a pause to take in the grandeur of this old seaport of Whitby. You look down from this elevated position on to the marina, the upper harbour with its myriads of craft of all types, to the old Whitby swing bridge. I find that it makes a perfect picture in the evening before the sun begins to set, sending out long-fingered shadows in a golden ethereal light.

Passing through the gap in the stone wall you are now back onto the road which leads to Windsor Terrace. It is now a matter of a quarter of a mile walk to bring you back to the point where you took your first steps when commencing your walk. You have now completed the Eskdale Way, not a long walk in comparison with some of the others, but if the weather has been kind I will guarantee that you have walked nowhere else that can have been more pleasurable. On this last day of your walk you will have covered about 18 miles and a total for the walk of 82 miles plus the mileage covered walking to accommodation and the return journey to get back on to the route.

Rail and Bus Services

NORTH YORKSHIRE MOORS RAILWAY
From Pickering, calling at Goathland and Grosmont. Enquiries to Commercial Manager, Pickering Railway Station, Pickering, YO18 8DA. Telephone: Pickering 72508 or 73535.

BRITISH RAIL
From Middlesbrough to Whitby, most trains calling at Kildale, Commondale, Castleton, Danby, Lealholm, Glaisdale, Egton Bridge and Grosmont. Connections can be made with the North Yorks Moors Railway at Grosmont.

Train service information from:
Middlesbrough 243208 (Weekdays, 08.00-21.00 hrs., and Sunday, 09.30-16.00 hrs.)
Whitby 602146 (Weekdays only, 08.30-18.00).

BUS SERVICES
I will show a few of the services coming in on the main routes into Whitby. Times of departure can be obtained from any United Automobile Services Limited bus station.

Middlesbrough — Newport Road, TS1 5AH. Telephone: Middlesbrough 247047.
Scarborough — Valley Bridge, YO11 2PD. Telephone: Scarborough 75463.
Whitby — Station Square, YO21 1DH. Telephone: Whitby 602146.

From Scarborough: 93, 93A, 93B, via Robin Hood's Bay and Hawsker.
257 and 258, via Sneaton and Ruswarp.

From Malton or Pickering: 92 via Goathland.

From Middlesbrough: 255 and 256 via Loftus.
257 and 258 via Aislaby, some buses call at Egton.

From Middlesbrough to Castleton and Danby No. 259, a very limited service.

Bibliography

Inside the North York Moors – Harry Mead. David and Charles, Newton Abbot.

The Priest of the Moors – Elizabeth Hamilton. Darton, Longman and Todd, London.

Whitby Lore and Legend – P. Shaw Jeffery. Published and Printed, Horne and Son Limited, Whitby.

Some Reminiscences and Folk Lore of Danby and District – Joseph Ford. Horne and Son Limited, Whitby.

Forty Years in a Moorland Parish – Rev. J. C. Atkinson. Macmillan and Company Limited, St. Martin's Street, London.

History of the Old Castle of Mulgrave – Hugh P. Kendall. A. Brown and Sons Limited, Hull.

The Manor, Lordship and Castle of Mulgrave – John Davison. Horne and Son Limited, Whitby.